Minibeasties and Their ADVENTURES

3: Mimi the Millipede

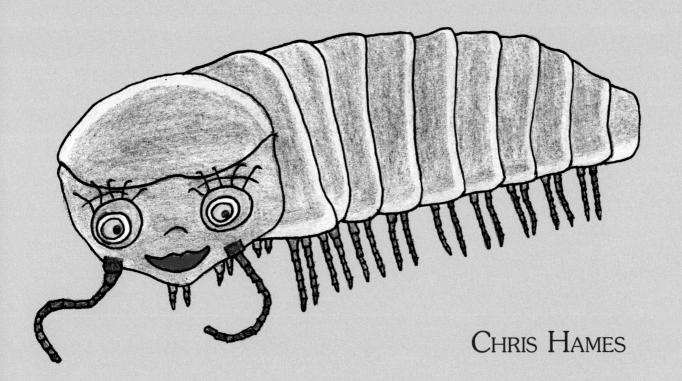

CHRIS HAMES

AuthorHouse™ UK
1663 Liberty Drive
Bloomington, IN 47403 USA
www.authorhouse.co.uk
Phone: 0800.197.4150

Published by AuthorHouse 11/30/2018

ISBN: 978-1-7283-8148-0 (sc)
ISBN: 978-1-7283-8147-3 (e)

authorHOUSE®

Dear Parents/Guardians,

Welcome to book 3
from the world of
Minibeasties!

This series of booklets is intended
to entertain children while providing
a positive learning experience. I
hope that you will find the books

informative and helpful in the development of literacy and numeracy skills.

While introducing elements of science alongside social awareness, they provide a range of activities to engage the child's imagination and enhance comprehension skills.

QR codes are included to provide links to more information about the animals. Please send feedback and or suggestions to Chris via minibeasties20@aol.com

Also in this series;
1: Woody the Woodlouse
2: Celine the Centipede

Thank you Freya Mennie, age
10, for drawing the birds and frogs on
page 18 and Sarah Taylor for support with
collating and proof reading.

v

Mimi lives in the wood. She likes to visit gardens.

2

Mimi likes to rest in dark, damp places, near to her food!

Mimi loves to eat fallen leaves—she likes all sorts of leaves, including mallow leaves.

6

Mimi has a lot of legs. 'Millipede' means 'a thousand legs' but she does not have that many. It looks as though she could have a hundred legs because she has two pairs of legs attached to each body segment. In fact she has eighteen (18) pairs of legs, which means she has eighteen lots of two (18 x 2), making thirty six (36) legs altogether.

Mimi will grow to two (2) centimetres long. She has a hard, mostly brown-coloured outer skeleton to protect her. She can fold her body into a ball shape for further protection. She is known as a 'Pill Millipede'.

Mimi's friend Mickey is a different type of millipede, who cannot fold his body into a ball. He can grow to more than 4cm long. For extra protection, he can release a nasty chemical which sends enemies away! Mickey has forty one (41) body segments, each with two (2) pairs of legs. This means that he has four (4) legs on each segment, and forty one lots of four (41 x 4) legs altogether, which means that he has 164 legs in total!

Mimi on the Mound

A short story

Mimi was tired. All of her thirty six legs were aching after climbing the steep hill. She was pleased though, that she had got to the top. The early morning view was lovely! Now she could rest her legs and enjoy the Spring day.

Mimi was munching at her morning meal of mallow leaves, when she heard a strange crashing sound. She looked around and saw her friend Mickey, but what was he doing?

"Hello Mimi," he called, "can you help me please?"

Mimi wondered what Mickey could want, and she still could not work out what was making the strange sound. Mickey was a good friend and Mimi would always be happy to help him. "Of course." She replied. "What can I do?"

"Well, I've joined the 'Musical Millipedes Marching Band', and they've asked me to practice banging the cymbals, but the trouble is that my legs are so close together that I keep tripping over the cymbals!"

Mimi looked at Mickey's legs and saw that he had a lot of cymbals attached to his front legs.

"Oh, I see." she said, and thought for a moment. An idea soon came to her. "Why don't I help you to take some cymbals from your front legs and put them on other legs further away? Then you'll have more control!"

Mickey agreed that this was a good idea, and before long he had cymbals evenly-spaced along his legs. He was so happy that he played all of them at once, making musical melodies across the meadow.

16

Soon, the birds, the crickets and even the frogs joined in, making a majestic musical dawn chorus.

Mimi moved her legs in rhythm while she munched her mallow leaves in time to the music. She was so happy that she curled herself into a ball and went rolling all the way back down the hill!

Colour Mimi's picture

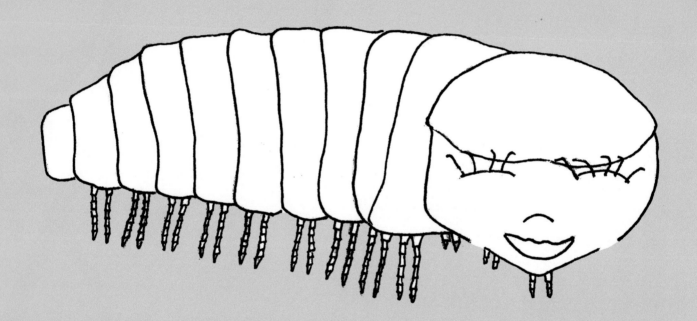

Can you add her eyes and antennae?

Quiz!

Where does Mimi live?

....

What does she like to do?

....

What does Mimi eat?

....

How many legs does she have?

....

What colour is Mimi?

....

How long is she?

....

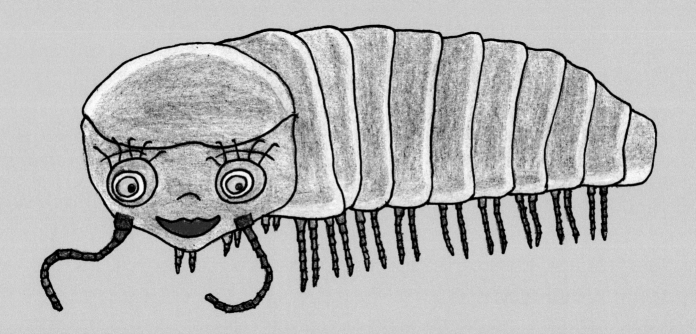

Mimi's Wordsearch

```
M  Z  A  W  P  D  M  M  C
B  I  Q  O  J  B  A  I  Y
L  S  M  O  G  A  L  C  M
W  O  H  I  L  L  L  K  B
A  A  W  Y  E  Q  O  E  A
M  O  U  N  D  P  W  Y  L
D  Y  L  E  F  T  E  R  W
M  I  L  L  I  P  E  D  E
```

Can you find these words in the wordsearch grid? MIMI, MICKEY, MALLOW, MILLIPEDE, MOUND, HILL, CYMBAL.

Poem

While Mimi munched on the mound

her friend Mickey wandered around.

He made such a clatter –

but it soon didn't matter,

when he made a more musical sound!

Cloze Passage

Can you find the correct places to put the missing words?

Mimi and Mickey are .... They met on the .... when Mickey made an unpleasant .... but after Mimi helped to move his .... he was able to join the marching.....................

(millipedes, mound, sound, cymbals, band)

Find out more about Mimi's family...

Mimi's Wordsearch Answers

M Z A W P D M M C

B I Q O J B A I Y

L S M O G A L C M

W O H I L L L K B

A A W Y E Q O E A

M O U N D P W Y L

D Y L E F T E R W

M I L L I P E D E

30

Printed in the United States
By Bookmasters